Walt Disney

SADDLEBACK
EDUCATIONAL PUBLISHING

Saddleback's Graphic Biographies

ISBN-10: 1-59905-230-X
ISBN-13: 978-1-59905-230-4
eBook: 978-1-60291-593-0

Printed in Craft Print International Ltd
NOR/0713/CA21301252

18 17 16 15 14   7 8 9 10 11

The name Walt Disney is known all over the world. He was the creator of Mickey Mouse and a pioneer* in the making of animated cartoons.

For millions of people who watched his weekly television program, he was an important part of something the family did together. He was a self-made man, and this is the story of how he did it.

He was born in Chicago in 1901, the fourth of five children. His father, Elias Disney, was working as a building contractor at the time.

His mother, Flora, was a school teacher before her marriage, but gave it up to raise her children.

* to originate or take part in the development of

When Walt was four years old, the family moved to a farm near Marceline, Missouri.

There was a lot of hard work to be done, and Elias made sure that his children did their share.

The two oldest boys didn't take to this new life. They ran away from home and went back to Chicago.

C'mon, Skinny!

Walt's best friend was his brother Roy. Roy was eight years older than Walt.

Look, Roy! I made this picture of Skinny!

That's great, kid!

Walt's father tried to make a living selling the apples from his two large orchards. After five years he knew he couldn't do it. He sold the farm and they moved to Kansas City.

In Kansas City, Disney bought a newspaper route of 2,000 people. Roy and Walt had to work for their father without pay. The other paperboys made three dollars a week.

Roy and Walt got up at 3:30 a.m. to deliver the morning paper.

Come on! Wake up!

I'll just rest here for a minute and get warm.

In winter, the snow was up to Walt's nose.

Brrrrr! It's cold!

When Walt woke up, he finished his deliveries and ran all the way to school.

He longed for the day when he wouldn't have to work for his father anymore.

A year went by. Roy finished high school and left home as his older brothers had done.

I wish I could go with you, Roy.

Me too, kid, but you've got to finish school.

Walt continued going to school and delivering papers. And on Saturdays he went to art classes at the Kansas City Art Institute.

Very good, Walt!

Sometimes in the evening, Elias Disney let his son go to the movies with a friend whose father owned a theater.

Why don't you wait?

The movies they saw were silent. The actors would move their lips to speak, and the audience could read what they were saying at the bottom of the screen.

Walt used some of the jokes he saw in the movies to put together an act for the local amateur shows.

In 1917, the year the United States entered World War I, Elias Disney sold the paper route and invested his money in a jelly factory in Chicago. When the family moved, Walt stayed behind to finish the school year.

That summer he worked as a "news butcher" on the Santa Fe Railroad.

Get your newspaper! Candy! Cold drinks!

In the fall he went to Chicago. He also worked in the jelly factory and took art classes at night.

One day, after school was out, Walt got a message from Roy. He was passing through Chicago on his way to a navy training camp and asked Walt to meet him at the train station.

Gee, kid! It's great to see you! You've gotten so tall!

They talked until the order was given for Roy and the other recruits* to board the train.

You there! On board! Train leaves in half a minute!

The officer had taken sixteen-year-old Walt for one of the recruits. It made him feel proud ... and it gave him an idea.

* a newly enlisted or drafted member of the armed forces

Walt knew you had to be eighteen to join the navy. He found out that the Red Cross Ambulance Corps took volunteers* at age seventeen.

Your name and age?

Walter Elias Disney, sir. Age seventeen.

Almost!

RED CROSS AMBULANCE CORP

There was one other problem. He needed one of his parents to sign the papers. His father wouldn't, but his mother gave in.

I'd rather know where you are than have you run off like the other boys.

The war ended while Walt was in Connecticut for training. Even so he was lucky enough to be sent to France for a year to deliver relief* supplies.

* a person who voluntarily undertakes or expresses a willingness to enter a service
* money, food, or other help given to those in need

Walt came back to the States in 1919. He headed for Kansas City to look for work as an artist.

His first job was at Gray's Advertising Company. There he met another young artist by the name of Ub Iwerks.

By December, both Walt and Ub and been laid off.

Why don't we start our own business? We could do ads and letterheads and things like that.

Sure! Why not?

A small newspaper gave them some office space in exchange for artwork. Walt bought supplies with money he had saved. They were in business!

We got two new ads today.

A few months later, they went out of business.

Walt and Ub were not doing well when they heard of a job opening at the Kansas City Film Ad Company.

Forty dollars a week! That's more than we both make together!

Why don't you take the job? I'll stay over here.

Disney convinced the company to hire Ub too.

At Kansas City Film Ad Company, Walt learned to make animated cartoons using cut-out figures with moveable parts.

In his spare time, he used a borrowed camera to make his own cartoons. A little later he sold these to a local theater.

These "laugh-o-grams" as he called them, used drawings instead of cutouts to create motion.

Soon Walt had enough money to start his own company, Laugh-O-Gram.

But within a year the company went bankrupt.

Walt ate once a day at a Greek restaurant where the owners gave him credit. At night he slept in the Laugh-O-Gram office.

Young Walt Disney was broke.

Finally, Walt sold his camera. He paid some of his debts and bought a train ticket to California. He wanted to get into the movie business. Also, his brother Roy was there recovering in a veteran's hospital.

In Los Angeles, he rented a room from his uncle, Robert Disney, and began looking for a job with a big motion picture company.

All he took with him from Kansas City were clothes and an unfinished animated short film called *The Alice Comedies* which had been made at Laugh-O Gram.

He didn't find one, so he rented an old camera and built an animation studio in his uncle's garage.

Finally, he found a buyer for *The Alice Comedies* renamed *Alice in Cartoonland*. He rushed to tell Roy.

A man from New York wants twelve *Alice* films, and he'll pay $1,500 a piece for them! How about it Roy? Will you go in on it with me?

When Roy was well, he and Walt borrowed five hundred dollars from their uncle, rented a tiny office, and set to work on the *Alice* films.

Roy had trouble cranking the old-fashioned movie camera at a steady pace.

Alice keeps speeding up and slowing down. Looks like we need a professional cameraman!

A real little girl was photographed against a simple backdrop. Then Walt would draw cartoons, which were photographed and printed on top of the live film.

Walt asked Ub Iwerks to move from Kansas City to Los Angeles to help with animation.

Hey, look who's here!

They made one *Alice* cartoon after another adding to the staff as they went along. The profits they made were used to buy better equipment and materials.

It's a good thing I like beans. We can't afford much else.

Walt and Roy rented an apartment together.

One new employee was a young woman named Lillian Bounds. Walt soon got in the habit of driving her home after work.

Are you sure you won't come in for a minute?

Walt was too ashamed of his old clothes to go in and meet Lillian's family.

Then one day ...

Roy, I'd like to take some money out of the business to buy a new suit.

By golly, I could use one too. You know Edna is moving out here, and we are going to get married!

At last Walt felt well enough dressed to call on Lillian at her home.

Their friendship grew. They even made plans to buy a car together. So when Walt found himself in need of a roommate after Roy and Edna were married ...

Well, Lilly, what do you think we should buy first: the car or the ring?

They were married in July 1925.

The company moved to a larger studio on Hyperion Avenue, and Walt and Lillian bought a house nearby.

After three years, *Alice in Cartoonland* lost its appeal and a new character was created.

Here he is boys, Oswald the Lucky Rabbit, for our new animated cartoons!

Oswald was quite popular.

We get $2,250 for each cartoon. But with all the work we put into them, it's not enough.

Taking Lillian with him, Walt made a trip to New York to ask for more money.

I'm sorry, Mr. Disney. I can only give you $1,800 for future *Oswald* cartoons.

I would lose money. It costs more than that to make!

I own Oswald the Lucky Rabbit! I have a contract signed by four of your artists who will work for me directly if you won't take my offer.

Walt would not take the contract. He was heartbroken that his employees would be disloyal to him.

From now on Lilly, I'll make sure that everything we create belongs to us.

Before boarding the train for Los Angeles, Walt sent a telegram to Roy.

How can you say that when you know it's not true?

I'll make it true!

By the time they reached the Midwest, Walt was feeling cheerful again. He was working on a new character instead of Oswald.

He's really cute but the name doesn't suit him at all.

MORTIMER MOUSE

Lillian had her way and the mouse was renamed "Mickey."

When Walt got back to the studio, work began right away on the new Mickey Mouse cartoons.

Soon afterwards, Warner Brothers released an important new movie called *The Jazz Singer*. It was the first talking picture that was a success.

Musician Wilfred Jackson created a musical score for a Mickey Mouse cartoon named *Steamboat Willie*.

The film ran at a rate of twenty-four frames per second using a metronome* to tick off two beats per second. The music was recorded after the animation was filmed. They were able to make the live action and music seem like a dance.

*an instrumental device which marks exact time by a ticking sound

After a long search, they found a company to record the soundtrack and an orchestra to play it. Walt himself did the voice of Mickey Mouse.

Steamboat Willie was a great success, and soon there were four Mickey Mouse cartoons with sound showing all over the country.

But as popular as Mickey Mouse was, Walt's distributor* tried to make Walt do something he didn't want to do. He said he would hire Ub Iwerks away from the Disney studio. Once again, Walt refused to be forced into a bad contract.

We'll just have to get another artist to do the mouse.

That guy doesn't realize that there is more to the success of Mickey Mouse than Ub's drawing. Part of it is your talent for telling the story and making the gags funny.

But a few years later, Ub came back to work for the Disney studio.

* an independent company that acts as an agent between a film production company and a movie theater

But Walt could not do one take. He wanted to be a success.

He was a perfectionist.* He was working too hard.

Do it over!

Finally, he went to a doctor. The doctor told him to take a long vacation.

When he returned to work, he was his old self again.

In the 1930s, the Disney studio grew very big. More people were added to the staff. Another thing that grew was Mickey Mouse's gang!

Pluto began in 1931. Goofy came a little later.

One day Walt heard a man named Clarence Nash on the radio. Nash recited "Mary Had a Little Lamb" in a duck voice.

* regards anything short of perfection as unacceptable

Walt got Mr. Nash to come to the studio and do his duck voice for the animators.

From that voice, they created Donald Duck, who made his first appearance in 1934.

Who, me? Oh, no! I got a bellyache!

CHIP and DALE

In the years that followed, Donald's three nephews joined the crew, as did Daisy Duck and the two chipmunks, Chip and Dale.

At the same time Disney made the Mickey Mouse cartoons, he was making films called *Silly Symphonies.*

In 1929 the first one showed a bunch of skeletons who rose from their graves and danced till dawn.

But three years before, in 1931, Disney had already won two Academy Awards. One of these was for a *Silly Symphony* called "Flowers and Trees" and the other was for creating Mickey Mouse.

Walt's most famous *Silly Symphony* was "The Three Little Pigs."

This was made at a time when many people were out of work.

18 MILLION JOBLESS: ROOSEVELT URGES AMERICANS TO STICK TOGETHER

THE THREE LITTLE PIGS

WALT DISNEY

Who's afraid of the big bad wolf, the big bad wolf, the big bad wolf ...

This happy song made the American people feel better. They sang it as the left the movie.

All the films took hard work. At twenty-four frames per second, a seven minute cartoon required about 10,000 drawings, each a little different from the one before it.

The main action was drawn by the animators, with assistant animators and "in-betweeners" filling in the rest of the drawings. Other jobs were done by layout and background men, directors, story men, and musicians.

One animator named Webb Smith, had a habit of pinning sketches on the wall by his desk. He did this so he could see the whole story at a glance.

Darn it, Webb. You're making holes in my nice new walls!

After thinking it over, Walt ordered cork boards so that all stories could be worked out this way. Thus the storyboard* was invented.

This is where Mickey ...

Meanwhile, Mickey Mouse's fame spread all over the world.

In 1935, the League of Nations gave Walt Disney a medal. They called Mickey Mouse an international symbol of good will.

So far, all the Disney films were "shorts." They were only shown in movie theaters before the "big" movie came on.

Yes, that's right! We plan to make a feature length cartoon based on the fairy tale "Snow White."

* series of illustrations or images displayed in sequence for the purpose of visualizing plot order and development

Snow White took five years to make. It cost $1,750,000. By 1937, the Disney staff had grown from 150 to 750 people.

There was a new kind of camera invented at the Disney studio. It was used for some of the scenes and gave the picture a new feeling of depth.

Many people called the project "Disney's Folly." Walt's faith in it was rewarded when *Snow White and the Seven Dwarfs* earned 8.5 million dollars on its first run (almost 100 million dollars today). Because of its success, Walt was able to go ahead with his next big project: a new studio.

By the time this studio was completed in 1940, the staff had grown again to 1,500 people.

The studio was comfortable and well equipped, but the company's growth brought new problems.

What bothers me is that some people get paid more than others for the same work.

The Screen Cartoonists Guild started a branch of its union in the Disney studio. On May 29, 1941, there was a strike.

During the strike, Walt made a "good will tour" of South America for the U.S. government.

In his absence, the strike was settled.

After the strike, Walt didn't feel as close to the people who worked for him. He spent more time with his wife and two daughters, Diane and Sharon.

During this time, Disney Studios created *Pinocchio, Fantasia,* and *Bambi.* With each of these films came new innovations.

Dad, read us a story. Please draw us a picture of Jiminy Cricket.

Okay, girls ... How about a drawing of Thumper?

When Walt took his daughters to amusement parks ...

We can create a park that is clean and fun for the entire family!

Walt's ideas for Disneyland began to form when Walt took his daughters to carousel and train rides on the weekends.

But then the United States entered World War II. Disney had to cut back on all his work. The United States Army used a part of his studio as a base for a seven-hundred-man anti-aircraft unit.

The army stayed for seven months. Then, for the next three years, the studio made educational films for the government. Not until after the war did work begin again on the new feature length cartoons, *Cinderella, Alice in Wonderland,* and *Peter Pan.*

On a trip to Alaska, Walt met two photographers named Elma and Al Milotte.

How would you like so do some movies of Alaska for me?

Of all the film the Milottes sent in, Walt liked the footage on the life of fur seals best.

The Milottes lived for a year in the Pribilof Islands doing just that.

The end result was an award-winning *True Life Adventure* called "Seal Island."

Shortly after the seals came the first live action film—with human actors, that is.

Treasure Island was filmed in England.

Then, to top off all his other work, Walt began to plan the amusement park of his dreams—Disneyland. This was in 1952.

It's the craziest idea I've ever heard of!

In order to raise support for Disneyland, Walt agreed to do a weekly television show called *Disneyland*.

Born on a mountain top in Tennessee ... ♫

The show's *Davy Crockett* series caused a national craze for coonskin caps.

A daily program called *Mickey Mouse Club* came next.

M-I-C-K-E-Y M-O-U-S-E

Besides the Mousketeers, the show had serials like "Spin and Marty" and, of course, the famous Disney cartoons.

Disneyland finally opened in 1955. The park was constructed with the same care that went into the studio's animation work. There were manmade waterways, shade trees, small-scale buildings, boats, and fanciful rides.

Mr. Disney, you must be a very wealthy man!

Yes, I guess I am; they tell me I owe about ten million dollars.

Walt made sure that it was kept clean and that park employees were cheerful and polite to all the guests.

Of the sixty-two feature films between 1950 and 1965, the biggest success was *Mary Poppins*.

It won five Academy Awards, bringing the total up to twenty-nine for Walt Disney Productions.

Disney's last project was Disney World. Built on 27,500 acres in Florida, it was to be much more than an amusement park.

Surrounding the park, we plan to build an experimental community of the future.

Toward the end of 1966, Walt Disney had to go into the hospital several times. Whenever he had visitors, Walt would talk to them about his plans for Disney World.

This is where we'll put the monorail ...

He died on December 15 at the age of 65.

But Walt Disney Productions goes on without Walt, as he would have wanted it to. As for that other Disney "gang," Mickey, Donald and the rest, they may be sure of a long and happy future in the hearts and eyes of many generations to come!